the GIFT of a MEMORY

Marianne Richmond

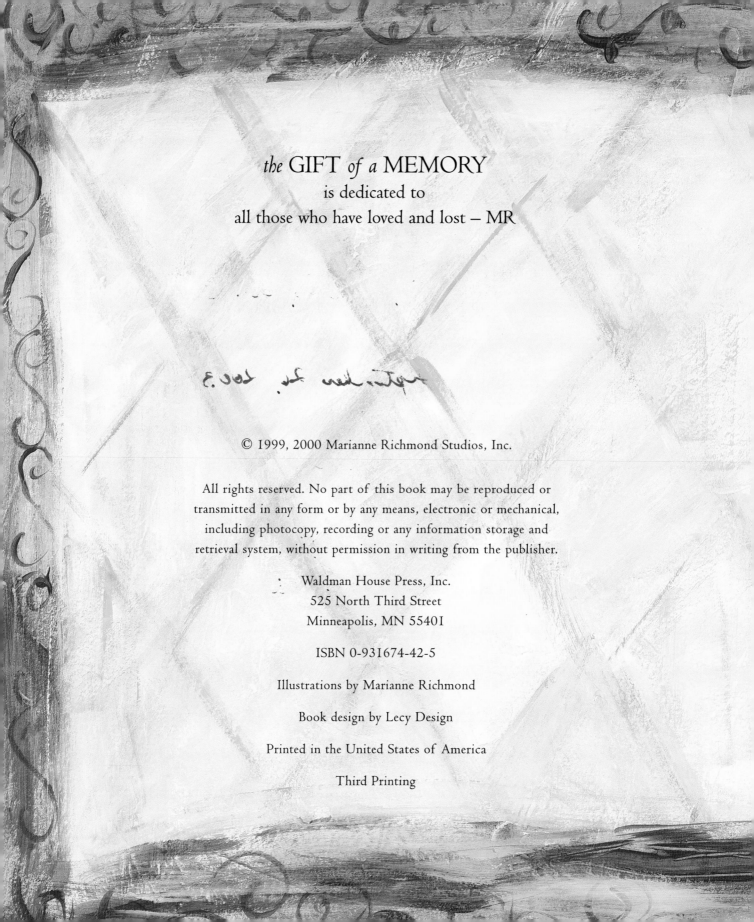

the GIFT *of a* MEMORY
is dedicated to
all those who have loved and lost – MR

Waldman House Press, Inc.
525 North Third Street
Minneapolis, MN 55401

ISBN 0-931674-42-5

Illustrations by Marianne Richmond

Book design by Lecy Design

Printed in the United States of America

Third Printing

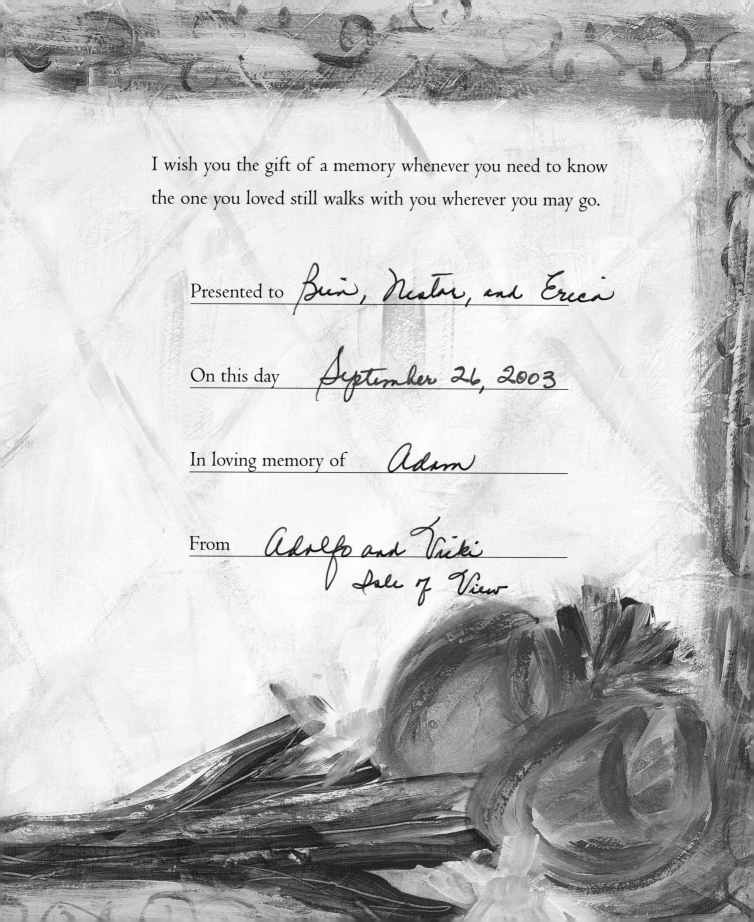

I wish you the gift of a memory whenever you need to know the one you loved still walks with you wherever you may go.

Presented to *Bin, Nestor, and Erica*

On this day *September 26, 2003*

In loving memory of *Adam*

From *Adolfo and Vicki*
Isle of View

SOME things seemed so usual

on that remembered day.

The sun arose, the birds awoke,

and kids came out to play.

For most of us, the hours passed

much like the days before.

We lost ourselves in busyness

and rushed from task to chore.

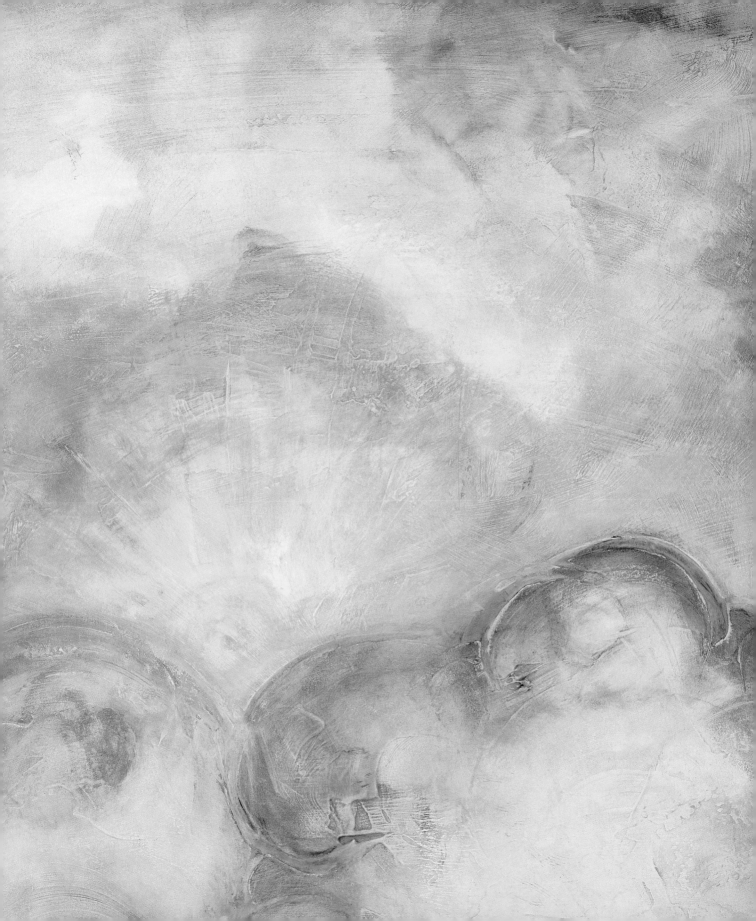

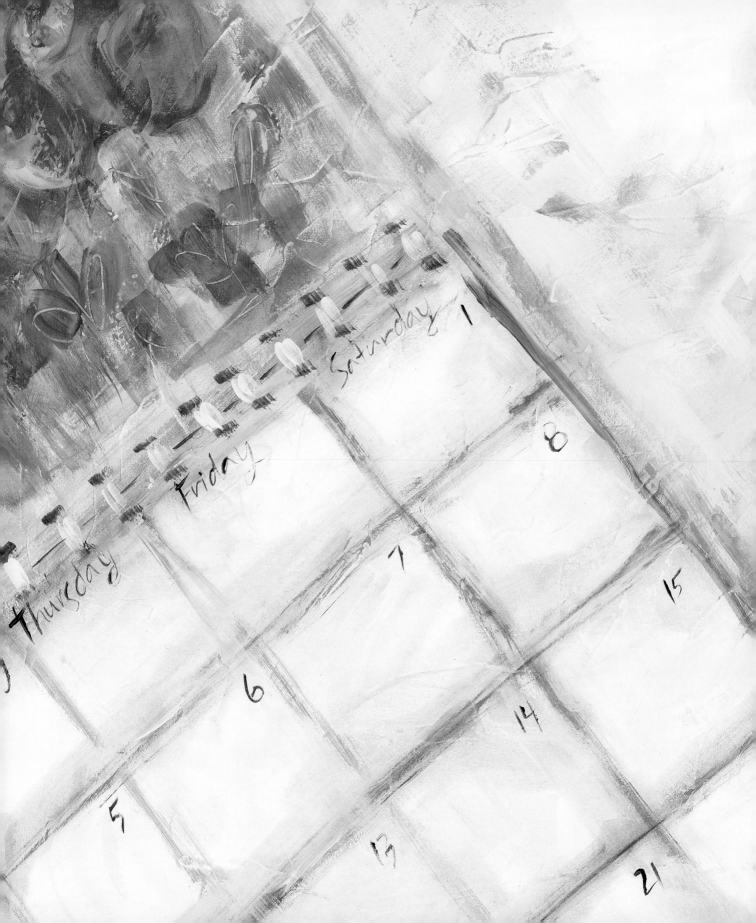

Thursday

Friday

Saturday 1

5

6

7

8

13

14

15

21

IT was not so for you, my friend,

and forever will it be

the day God said to your beloved,

"Come home and dwell with me."

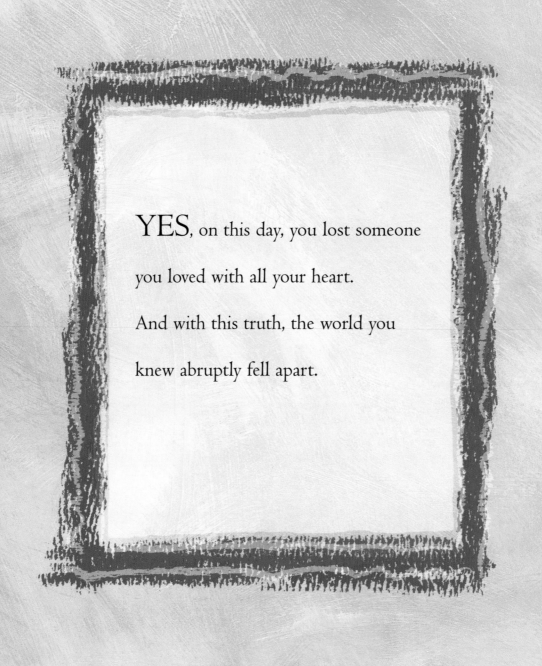

YES, on this day, you lost someone

you loved with all your heart.

And with this truth, the world you

knew abruptly fell apart.

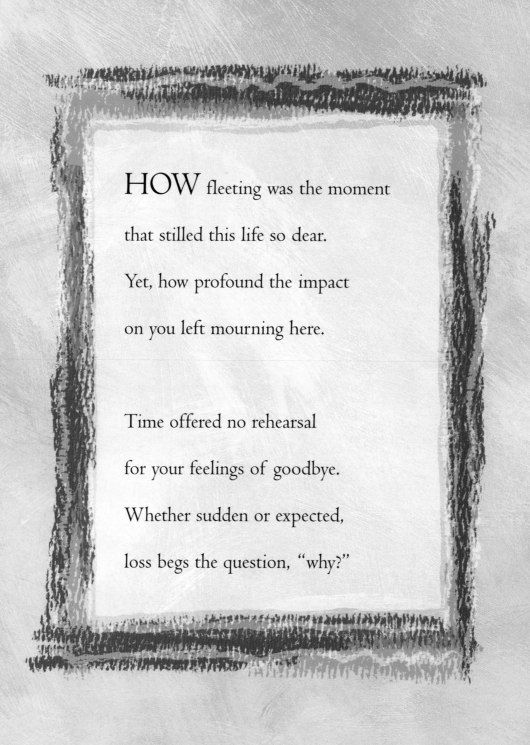

HOW fleeting was the moment

that stilled this life so dear.

Yet, how profound the impact

on you left mourning here.

Time offered no rehearsal

for your feelings of goodbye.

Whether sudden or expected,

loss begs the question, "why?"

SOME say God sends His children here

with special tasks to do,

then calls them to Him, one by one,

when all their work is through.

OTHERS feel, "Thy will was done,"

in life's eternal plan. And when we enter

heaven's gates, we'll finally understand.

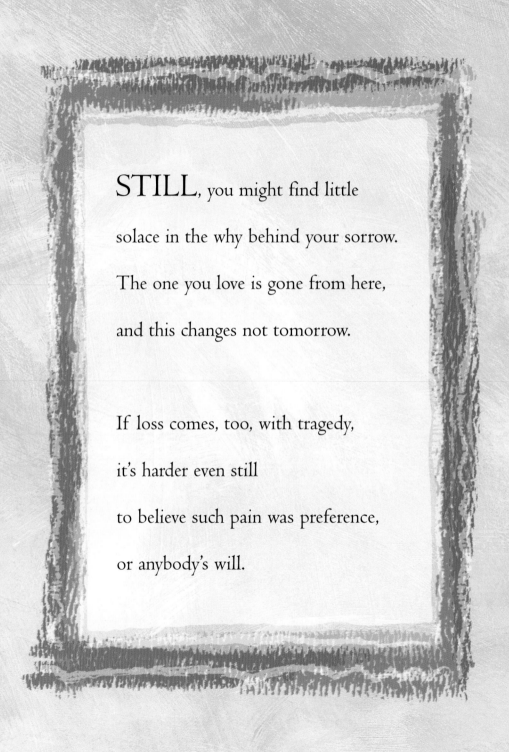

STILL, you might find little

solace in the why behind your sorrow.

The one you love is gone from here,

and this changes not tomorrow.

If loss comes, too, with tragedy,

it's harder even still

to believe such pain was preference,

or anybody's will.

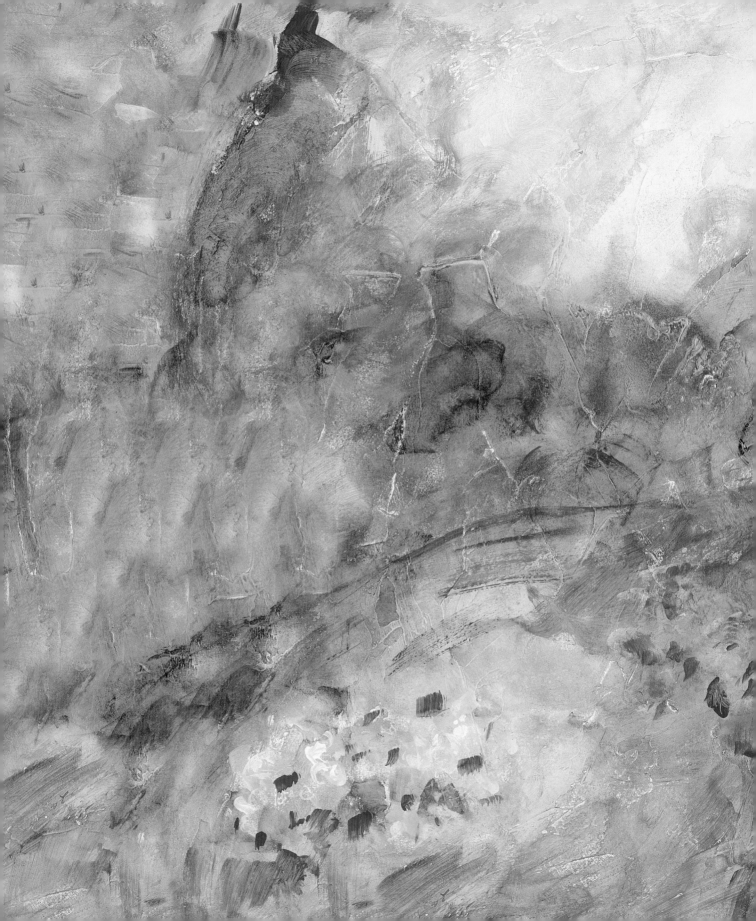

WITH this, your heart does lead

you along a path of grief, where you

gather precious memories, and

through tears you find relief.

THE pace at which you travel is

yours to set and share with those on whom

you'll count to listen, talk, and care.

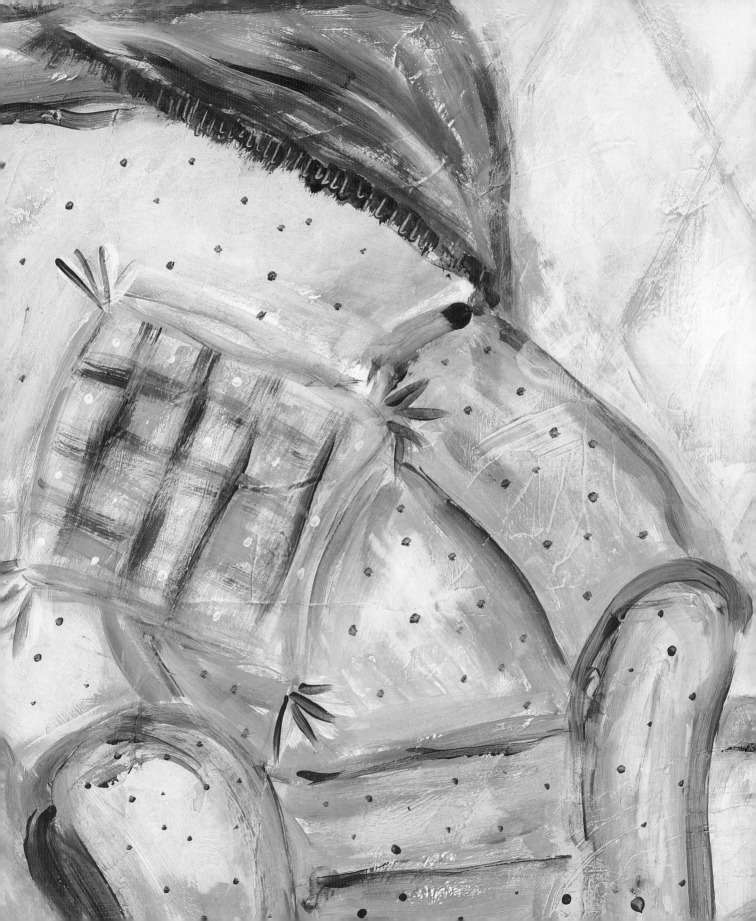

YOU may wish yourself to hurry

and believe your mourning through,

but pain from loss prefers to stay

and make a home in you.

AND there it will become a friend

who gently helps you cross

into a life that finds new meaning

from your encounter with such loss.

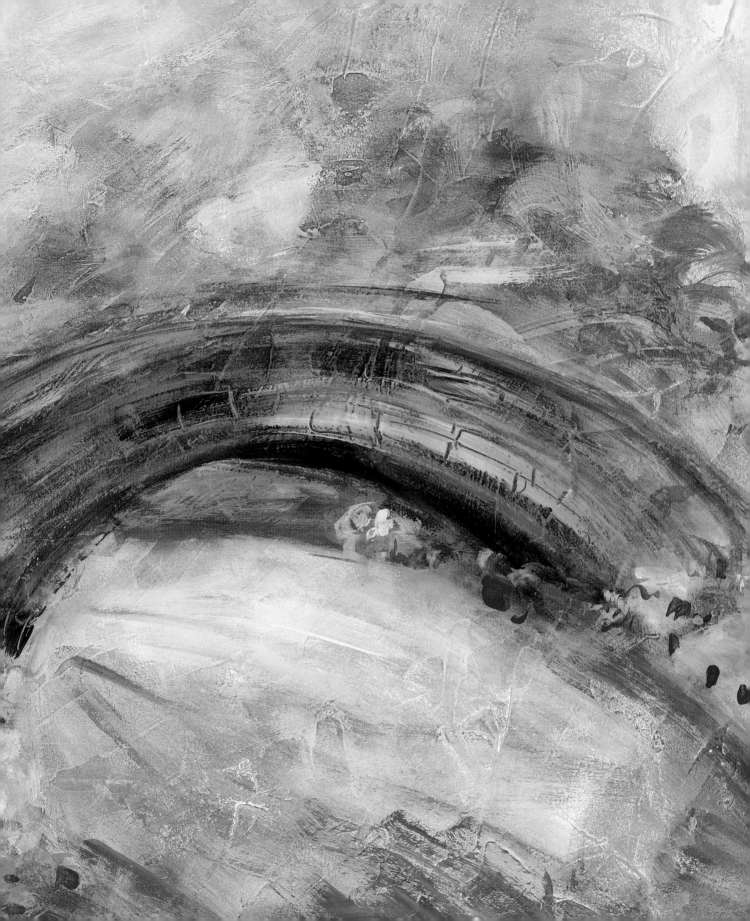

THIS healing happens slowly

over weeks and months and years.

And even then, there will be days

when memories call fresh tears.

A song, a scent, or photograph
keeps your heart in touch
with all that you so treasured
in the one you miss so much.

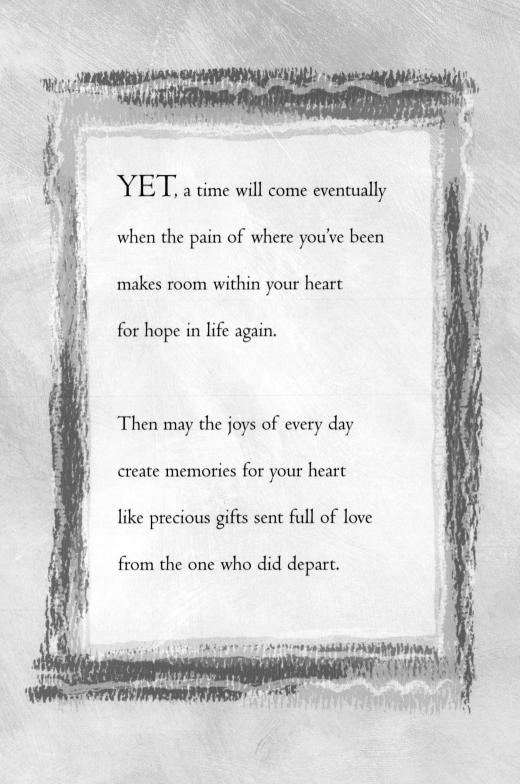

YET, a time will come eventually

when the pain of where you've been

makes room within your heart

for hope in life again.

Then may the joys of every day

create memories for your heart

like precious gifts sent full of love

from the one who did depart.

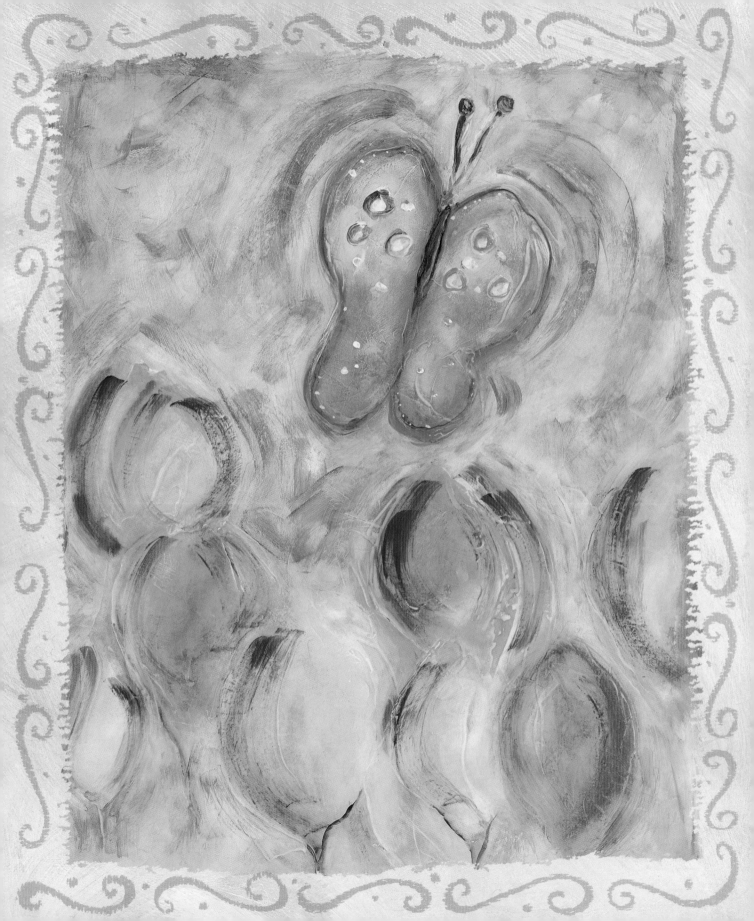

MAY you sense your loved one's

spirit on a lazy sunshine day

and know the one you miss delights

to watch you laugh and play.

MAY you recall that radiant smile

in the sparkle of a star

and know it's shining extra bright

to find you from afar.

MAY you hear your beloved's

laughter in the misty falling rain

and know that tears from heaven fall

from eyes that share your pain.

MAY you feel your loved one's touch

when mild breezes blow...

TO caress your cheek and whisper soft,

"I still walk with you, you know."

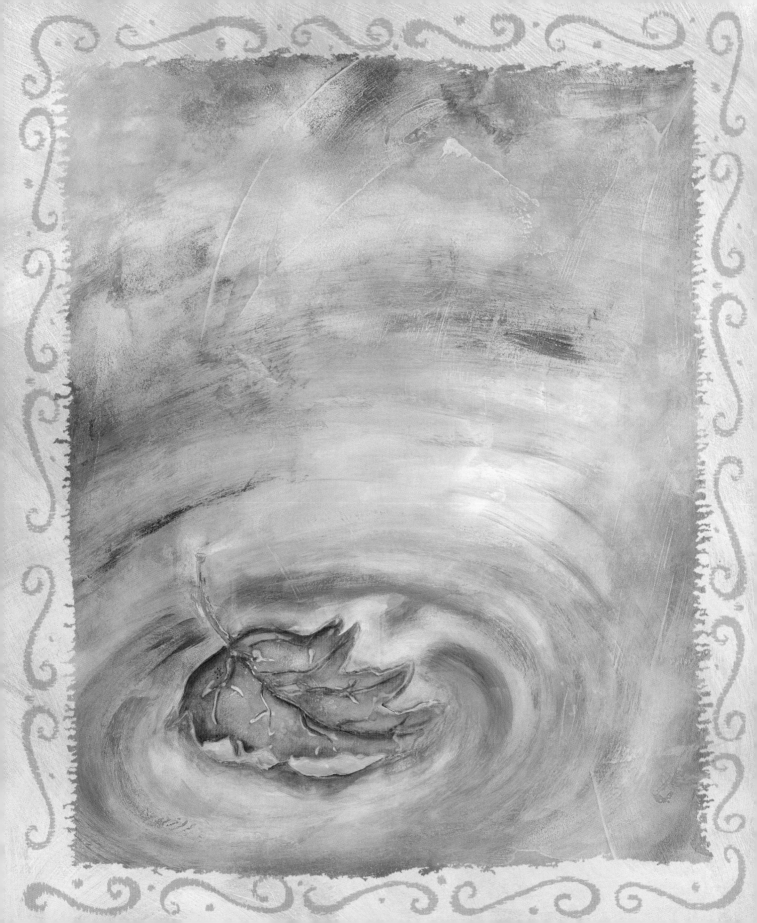

SPECIAL MEMORIES

_____

_____

_____

_____

_____

_____

_____

_____

_____

_____

_____

_____

_____

_____

_____

_____